Animal Parents

Elspeth Graham

OXFORD

UNIVERSITY PRESS

Great Clarendon Street, Oxford OX2 6DP

Oxford University Press is a department of the University of Oxford.
It furthers the University's objective of excellence in research, scholarship,
and education by publishing worldwide in

Oxford   New York

Auckland Cape Town Dar es Salaam Hong Kong Karachi
Kuala Lumpur Madrid Melbourne Mexico City Nairobi
New Delhi Shanghai Taipei Toronto

With offices in

Argentina Austria Brazil Chile Czech Republic France Greece
Guatemala Hungary Italy Japan Poland Portugal Singapore
South Korea Switzerland Thailand Turkey Ukraine Vietnam

Oxford is a registered trade mark of Oxford University Press
in the UK and in certain other countries

British Library Cataloguing in Publication Data

Data available

ISBN 978-0-19-846107-4

13 15 17 19 20 18 16 14 12

Printed in China

Paper used in the production of this book is a natural,
recyclable product made from wood grown in sustainable forests.
The manufacturing process conforms to the environmental
regulations of the country of origin

Acknowledgements

The publisher would like to thank the following for permission to reproduce photographs: **p4** Robert
Pickett/Corbis UK Ltd.; **p5**t Alamy/Stephen Frink collection, b Animals Animals/Earth Scenes/Photolibrary Group;
p6t Tony Hamblin/Frank Lane Picture Agency, b Michael & Patricia Fogden/Frank Lane Picture Agency; **p7**t John
R. MacGregor/Still Pictures, b By Ian Miles-Flashpoint Pictures/Alamy; **p8** Katherine Feng/Globio/Minden
Pictures/Frank Lane Picture Agency; **p9**t Theo Allofs/Zefa/Corbis UK Ltd., b Joe McDonald/Corbis UK Ltd.; **p10**t
Science Photo Library; b Nature Picture Library; **p11**t Jonathan Blair/Corbis UK Ltd., b Photolibrary Group; **p12**t
Frans Lanting/Minden Pictures/Frank Lane Picture Agency, b Animals Animals/Earth Scenes/Photolibrary Group;
p13t Photolibrary Group, b Daniel L. Geiger/SNAP/Alamy; **p14**t Rob Howard/Corbis UK Ltd., b Kevin
Schafer/Corbis UK Ltd.; **p15**t Daniel H. Janzen, b Treat Davidson/Frank Lane Picture Agency; **p16** Peter
Johnson/Corbis UK Ltd.; **p17**t The Nation/AFP/Getty Images, b Dr. Ron Cohn/The Gorilla Foundation/Koko.org;
p18l Mike Jones/Frank Lane Picture Agency; r Oxford Scientific Films; **p19**t Bruce Coleman Inc./Frank Lane
Picture Agency, b Bruce Lyon; **p20**t Daniel J. Cox/Corbis UK Ltd., b Hal Beral/Corbis UK Ltd.; **p21**t Tui De
Roy/Minden Pictures/Frank Lane Picture Agency, b Linda Lewis/Frank Lane Picture Agency; **p22**t Darren
Whiteside/Reuters/Corbis UK Ltd., b Ardea/Jean-Paul Ferrero; **p23**t Animals Animals/Earth Scenes/Photolibrary
Group, b Wil Meinderts/Foto Natura/Frank Lane Picture Agency.s Animals/Earth Scenes/Photolibrary Group

Cover: FLPA/Fritz Polking

Contents

Who cares?

Different baby animals get different kinds of care from their parents. Some babies get care from both parents. Some are raised by just one parent. Some parents don't play any role in their **offspring's** life at all.

Newborn turtles never know their parents. The tiny turtles **fend** for themselves.

Many insects, fish, frogs and turtles put their energy into producing lots of eggs. They put little or no energy into looking after their young. Out of the large numbers of eggs that they lay, the chances are that at least a few of the young will survive and grow into adults.

The sunfish lays as many as 300 million tiny eggs at a time.

Other parents produce very few offspring in their lifetime. They put their energy into caring for their young. Elephants have few babies and are very caring parents.

Animal	How long parental care lasts
elephant calves	at least 5 years
bear cubs	2 years
alligator hatchlings	about a year
kangaroo joeys	9 months
black-headed ducklings	a few hours
turtle hatchlings	none

A pair of parents

Most birds share parental care. Both parents can help build the nest and either bird can sit on the eggs. Young birds eat food that can be collected by both parents.

Sometimes parents share all the tasks, sometimes they have particular roles.

Bullfinches share all the parenting.

The male hornbill's role is to feed his family.

Hornbills nest in hollows. After the female lays her eggs, the male seals the nest up to keep his family safe. He only leaves a small slit that he can poke his beak through.

North American prairie voles **mate** for life and raise their young together. The male vole helps with the birth of the young and both parents raise the **litter**. They groom and cuddle their babies.

Scientists have discovered that male prairie voles have a special **gene** that makes them stay with one partner for life.

Marmosets are always on the move searching for food. The father's role is to carry the young until the mother returns to feed them. This leaves the mother free to find enough food to feed herself and make enough milk to feed her babies.

Marvellous mothers

Most parenting care comes from the mother. Many mothers raise their young alone.

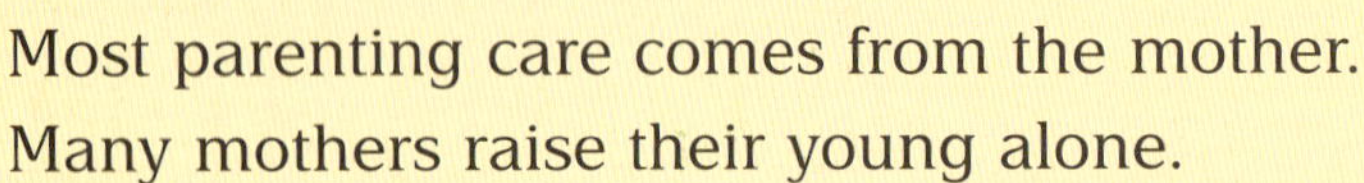

The mother panda weighs almost a thousand times more than her baby.

The giant panda gives birth to the tiniest cub. The cub is born blind and helpless and it has a very loud piercing cry, a bit like a human baby. The panda is a very attentive mother; she carries her baby gently in her mouth everywhere she goes for the first few weeks.

A baby kangaroo is only about
2.5 centimetres long when it is
born. It crawls up to its mother's
pouch where it lives and feeds
on its mother's milk. When the
young kangaroo, or joey, is about
6 months old it leaves the pouch
for short periods of time. It
jumps back in when it wants to
feed or feel safe. Eventually the
mother decides not to let the
joey back in, so then it must
become independent.

The joey lives in its mother's
pouch for about 9 months.

The tiny scorpions stay on their
mother's back for about two weeks.

Female scorpions carry
their eggs in a pouch.
When they hatch the
young crawl out and
climb up onto their
mother's back.

Usually, a manatee gives birth to a single calf. At once the mother swims underneath the calf and helps it to the surface where it takes its first gulp of air. The calf drinks its mother's milk when it is underwater. Sometimes the mother seems to cradle her baby with a flipper.

The manatee calf stays with its mother for about 2 years.

A shrew family travels in a line. The mother is at the front and each baby shrew holds on by its teeth to the tail of the one in front. They break up to feed and explore, and then re-form the line at any hint of danger.

A mother crocodile can carry about a dozen hatchlings at a time.

A crocodile lays her eggs in the sand. She waits until she hears tiny cries coming from the eggs. Then she digs them up and helps her babies to hatch. She throws them into the air and catches them in her jaws. She holds them in a pouch at the bottom of her mouth and carries them to a safe place near the river.

Young alligators ride on their mother's head where they sometimes wriggle and put their feet in her eyes.

Fantastic fathers

The female emperor penguin lays an egg and passes it to the male who balances it on his feet. The female then goes off to feed. The father penguin stands in a tight **huddle** with other male penguins, all balancing eggs on their feet.

The father penguins stand for about 2 months in freezing **Antarctic** temperatures until the eggs hatch.

The male seahorse has a pouch in which the female lays her eggs. She then swims off and leaves him. After 2 months the baby seahorses hatch and leave his pouch.

The father takes care of the baby seahorses until they can fend for themselves.

The female Darwin's frog lays eggs on the forest floor.
The male watches over the eggs until the tadpoles
start to move. Then he appears to swallow them.
He actually keeps them in a pouch in his mouth.

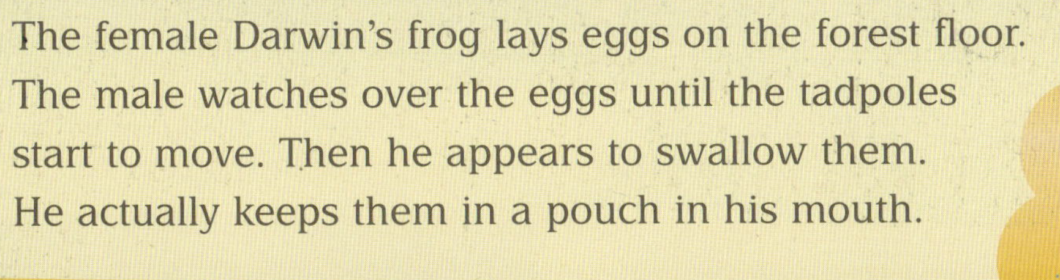

When the tadpoles turn into
tiny frogs they jump out of
their father's mouth.

The giant water bug cements her eggs
onto the male's back. The eggs are an
awkward and heavy load.

With his load of eggs, the
father water bug can't
feed and finds it hard to
escape his **predators**.

Baby minding

Mother giraffes give birth standing up so baby giraffes enter the world with a six foot drop! When the young giraffes are about 4 weeks old they are gathered together in groups called crèches. One mother looks after all the calves while the other mothers go off and graze.

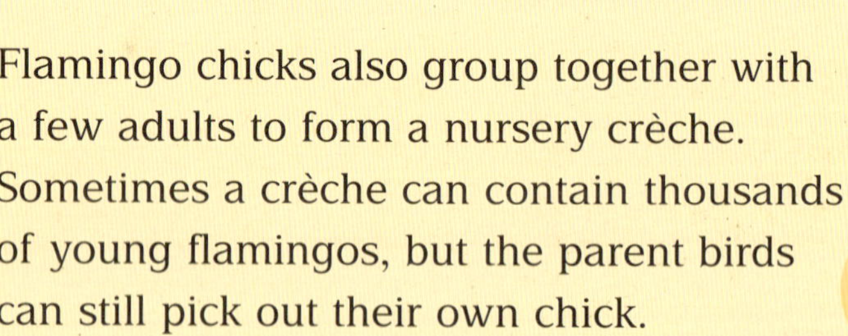

Flamingo chicks also group together with a few adults to form a nursery crèche. Sometimes a crèche can contain thousands of young flamingos, but the parent birds can still pick out their own chick.

Fantastic fact!
The fossils of a mother dinosaur and 34 young were recently discovered in China. Scientists believe this is evidence of a dinosaur crèche.

Rufous wrens use wasps to help protect their offspring. The birds build their nests next to wasps' nests. If a predator, like a snake, monkey or other intruder, comes too close, the wasps will attack.

The queen bee lays all the eggs in the hive. But the eggs and **larvae** are cared for by special nurse bees.

The nurse bees visit each individual larva about 1300 times a day!

Adoptive parents

Some animals will raise another animal's young. This kind of adoption is most common in animals that live in **colonies**, like seals, bats and gulls.

When a pair of ostriches with chicks meets another pair with chicks they often fight. The winning parents chase the other parents away and eagerly gather their chicks in with their own brood. Very aggressive ostrich parents sometimes end up with several hundred chicks!

Occasionally, animals adopt the offspring of different **species**. A raccoon has been seen raising a kitten along with her own babies. Dogs with young puppies have also suckled kittens, and cats have raised baby rats.

Recently in Kenya, Africa, a lioness took in and cared for a newborn baby oryx.

Koko is a gorilla. She loves kittens and cares for them in the same way a gorilla cares for her babies. When her first kitten, All Ball, was killed by a car, Koko **mourned** and cried for months. Because she was the first gorilla to learn sign language, she was able to ask for a new kitten, and chose one that looked like All Ball.

A stranger in the nest

Some birds avoid the bother of parenting altogether by laying their eggs in other birds' nests.

The adoptive parents nearly always care well for the baby birds. Usually they don't suspect that these chicks aren't theirs – even if the chick is so big that the adoptive parent has to sit on its shoulder to be able to feed it!

Cuckoos lay eggs that look like the eggs that belong in the nest.

The cuckoo steals an egg from another bird's nest and then replaces it with one of its own.

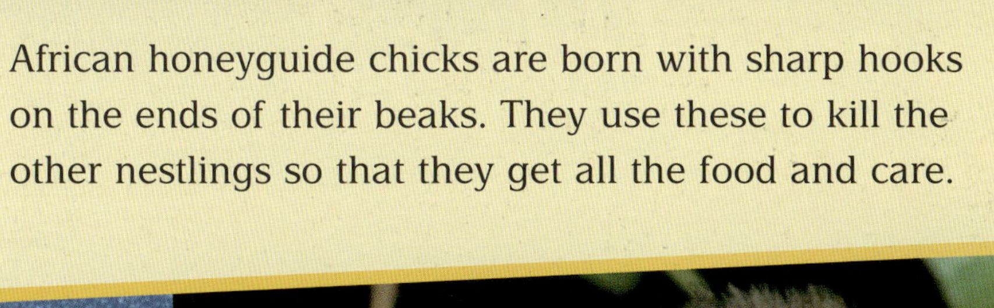

African honeyguide chicks are born with sharp hooks on the ends of their beaks. They use these to kill the other nestlings so that they get all the food and care.

The black-headed duck also lays its eggs in the nests of other birds. But the baby ducklings aren't too much trouble to their new parents. Only a few hours after they hatch the ducklings leave the nest and are completely independent.

Here's something I ate earlier

Mammals feed their young with milk. Polar bears have very rich milk so that their cubs grow very fast.

Other creatures provide their young with special liquid foods.

The female hummingbird carries **nectar** in a sac in her throat and **regurgitates** it into the open beaks of her young.

Pelicans regurgitate partly **digested** food back into their throats. The young reach far into their parents' beaks to feed.

Young pelicans take their food from their parent's open beak.

Fantastic fact!

The first thing a mother grebe (a water bird) feeds her chicks is feathers. The feathers line the chick's stomach and stop sharp fish bones damaging its delicate gut.

Both male and female discus fish produce a sort of nutritious slime on their bodies to feed their young.

Pigeons **digest** their food completely and then make a **secretion** that is called 'pigeon milk' with which they feed their young. It looks more like cottage cheese than milk and is very **nutritious**.

Keeping clean

Many female mammals lick their offspring clean as soon as they're born. This helps the babies breathe and dries their fur. It also helps the mother **bond** with her young.

Primates lick, nibble and pick with their fingers to keep their young clean.

Elephant mothers use their trunks to shower their calves, and then they dust them down and pat them dry with their trunks.

Many animals lick up the droppings of their young for the first few weeks and keep both the babies and their dens or nests clean.

Birds have to be very careful about cleaning up after their chicks. Streaks of white **excrement** would show predators where the nest is.

Some chicks produce fecal sacs – little packages of excrement – which many adult birds happily swallow. As the chicks get older the parent bird is more likely to carry the fecal sac away from the nest and dump it.

Who cares the best?

Different parents care for their young in very different ways. The parents of all species of animals do whatever works best for them, but are some parents better at caring than other parents? Are there any bad parents? What do you think?

Glossary

Antarctic – to do with Antarctica – the coldest continent on Earth

bond – become attached to

colonies – numbers of one type of animal that live close together in an organised way

digest – the way food is broken down and absorbed by the body

excrement – waste matter cast out from the body

fend – to manage without help

genes – units within every living creature that determine how they look and behave

huddle – a tightly packed group or crowd

larvae – the newly hatched, often wormlike, form of many insects

litter – a number of young animals born at one time

mammals – animals that have hair or fur and feed their young with milk

mate – become a pair for breeding

mourn – to feel sorrow for a loss

nectar – a sweet liquid found in plants

nutritious – providing goodness for the body

offspring – the young of an animal

predator – an animal that feeds on other animals

primates – a group of animals including monkeys, apes, gorillas and chimpanzees

regurgitate – to bring food that has been swallowed back up into the mouth

secretion – a special substance made by the body

species – groups of related living things

Quiz

Can you find the answers to these in the book?

Who looks after newborn turtles?

What sort of animal is a joey?

Where do baby scorpions live for the first two weeks of their lives?

Who throws her babies in the air and catches them in her jaws?

Where do rufous wrens like to build their nests?

Why does a mother grebe feed her chicks feathers?

How do mother elephants keep their calves clean?